A Selection of Popular Japanese Recipes

A TASTE OF JAPAN

Published by:
Publications Division, South China Morning Post Ltd.,
Tong Chong Street, Quarry Bay, Hong Kong.
in association with:
Four Corners Publishing Co. (Far East) Ltd.,
Suite 15A, 257 Gloucester Road, Hong Kong.

Copyright © 1981, Kenneth Mitchell

ISBN 962 224 003 8

Typeset by Filmset Ltd., Hong Kong.
Printed in Hong Kong.

Introduction

No pun is intended when stating that the very essence of Japanese cuisine is simplicity; in content, in preparation and in presentation. This is not to imply that the serving of a Japanese meal is an easy matter. On the contrary. The very 'simplicity' itself is time-consuming and requires the sensibility of an artist as much as the instinct of a cook. The uncluttered table setting, the careful choice of serving vessels and the general ambiance being as important as the delicate arrangement and aromatic flavour of the food.

Of prime importance in every Japanese kitchen is the freshness of the ingredients and cooking time is generally minimal. Many restaurants tend to consist of a simple bar, or counter, with the chefs on one side and the diners on the other. This method of serving not only helps to lend a colourful atmosphere but, most important, enhances the freshness and natural goodness of the food. Very often such establishments specialise in one type of 'dish' and the a la carte menu tends to be used less in Japan than elsewhere. When planning to eat out, therefore, the question 'WHAT?' usually precedes 'WHERE?'. It is only after a preference for the type of food has been settled that one decides where to go for the chosen Sushi, Tempura, Soba, Yakitori, Teppanyaki, Unagi or whatever.

Without doubt, and I believe with every justification, the best known of all the Japanese culinary delights are the raw fish delicacies, Sashimi and Sushi. Yet, ironically, nothing tends more to cause many foreigners to shy away from all Japanese food. Such people make two bad errors of judgement. Firstly, while it is true that fish (both raw and cooked) constitute a very important part of the national diet it is still only a part of the over-all culinary scene. Chicken, pork, noodles and vegetables all have a tasty and nutritious role to play as does the local beef (considered by many to be the finest in the world), providing, as it does, such dishes as Teppanyaki, Sukiyaki and Shabu-Shabu to excite even the most jaded palates. The second error can most easily be expressed by the use of the old adage: "If you haven't tried it, don't knock it". For I've found that the voice that protests loudest about the idea of eating raw fish is most generally the voice of total inexperience. I suggest that, once tried, a meal of selected Sashimi (carefully cut slices of a variety of seafood) and Sushi (the same, served on small beds of vinegared rice), served with cups of delicious warm saki, will always remain in the memory as an unequaled gastronomic experience.

A fine example of THE TASTE OF JAPAN where the freshest of food is cooked while the diner looks on.
Photographed at the **Inaka-ya,** a Japanese country-style restaurant located in the heart of Tokyo.

In the Western world, Japanese cuisine has, in the past, tended to take second place to its universally popular Chinese counterpart with the result that certain necessary ingredients have often been difficult to find. However, over recent years its popularity has grown and this is no longer the case. All ingredients mentioned in this edition should prove easily obtainable, particularly in the larger cities. Some substitutions have been offered and, in most cases, for the sake of simplicity, the English name has been used in the recipes. For the benefit of those readers interested, however, a brief glossary of terms is included. The recipes herein are mostly for 4–6 servings and as most were obtained from professional chefs, more used to cooking for large gatherings, certain deliberate changes have been made, as with other books in this series, to give a more practical application for the domestic kitchen. Naturally, space has only permitted the inclusion of a cross section of the many recipes available but still sufficient, I sincerely hope, to encourage you to develop a liking for the wonderfully different TASTE OF JAPAN.

Weights and Measures

Most of the weights and measures throughout the book are in metric but any ingredient under 25 grams (25 g) or 25 millilitres (25 ml) has been indicated in teaspoons. For those who continue to think and work in Imperial measures there is a quick and simple conversion to keep in mind. That is to take 25 grams as being equal to 1 ounce and 25 millilitres to 1 fluid ounce. However this is not a precise conversion and, while quite satisfactory for small quantities, tends to become less practical as weights and measures increase. The table opposite shows the nearest gram/millilitre equivalent for 1 to 20 ounces/fluid ounces and indicates the difference between the Imperial and U.S. pint. A measuring cup is roughly the equivalent of 225 millilitres.

Ounces/fluid ounces	Approx. g. and ml. to nearest whole figure	Ounces/fluid ounces	Approx. g. and ml. to nearest whole figure
1	28	11	311
2	57	12	340
3	85	13	368
4	113	14	396
5	142	15	428
6	170	16 (American pint)	456
7	198	17	484
8	226	18	512
9	255	19	541
10	283	20 (Imperial pint)	569

Kenneth Kiddell

Glossary

ABURAGE	Fried bean curd, usually sold in frozen sheets. Can be kept frozen for several months.
AZUKI	Red soy-beans, usually used for desserts. Sold in cans.
DAIKON	Very large variety of white radish. Turnip can be substituted.
GOMA	Sesame seeds. Must be roasted in a hot pan until they start "popping". Can then be used as garnish or ground into a paste and used as flavouring.
KAMABOKO	Japanese fish sausage. Sold in cans and usually is sliced for use.
KATSUOBUSHI	Dried bonito flakes, sold in packets. Used as garnish or flavouring for soups, etc..

KOMBU	Kelp-like seaweed, sold in dried, black ribbon form. Generally used as flavouring for dashi or sushi rice, but also pickled and used as a relish. Can be stored indefinitely.
MATSUTAKE	Japanese mushrooms with a most distinctive flavour. Quite hard to find and therefore expensive. There is no real substitute, although shiitake or other mushrooms can be used, but the authentic flavour will be lost.
MISO	Paste made from soy-beans. Used as a soup base, mixed with dashi. Sold in packets.
MIRIN	Japanese sweet rice wine, used only for cooking. A cooking sherry or white wine may be substituted.
MITSUBA	Watercress
NORI	Dried laver, shiny purple in colour and sold in paper-thin sheets. Must be warmed and crisped before use. Used as garnish and flavouring for soups. Spinach may be substituted in most cases.
SAKE	Japanese rice wine. Usually served hot in small cups as an accompaniment to a meal or as an aperatif, but also used in cooking quite frequently.
SHIITAKE	Japanese mushrooms, usually sold dried in packets and must be reconstituted before use.
SHIRATAKI	Japanese translucent noodles, sold in packets or cans and ready for use.
TAKENOKO	Bamboo shoots, sold in cans, water-packed. After removal from can, can be stored in fresh water in refrigerator for up to 10 days.
TOFU	Custard-like soy-bean cake and a staple in many Japanese dishes. Sold in squares or cubes. High source of protein.
TOGARISHI	Seasoning made from black pepper and other spices. Black or red (hot) pepper may be substituted.
WAKAME	Seaweed, sold in dry strands. Must be soaked before use. Used in soups for flavouring or as a vinegared relish. Spinach can usually be substituted.
WASABI	Green horseradish, with a particularly hot flavour. Sold in a dried, powdered form and must be mixed with water to form a paste. Hot mustard can be substituted.

Dashi *(basic Japanese soup stock)*

2 litres cold water
8 cm square Kombu (kelp seaweed)
50 g dried bonito flakes

In a large saucepan, bring the water to a rapid boil. Wash the seaweed under cold running water and add to the boiling water. Lower heat, allow to simmer for 2–3 minutes, then remove and discard the seaweed and add the bonito flakes. Stir well and bring the water back to the boil, then immediately, remove pan from heat and allow the flakes to settle to the bottom. Pour through a fine strainer, or cheesecloth, into a bowl. The stock is ready for immediate use or may be stored in a refrigerator for up to 48 hours.

Miso Soup *(bean paste soup)*

2 squares tofu (bean curd), about 200 g
2 spring onions
1 litre dashi
75 g miso (red bean paste)
salt to taste

Cut the tofu into small dice and finely chop the spring onions. Pour most of the stock into a saucepan and bring to the boil. Rub the bean paste through a fine sieve into the boiling stock, using the remaining stock to help press it all through. Add the diced tofu, lower heat, add salt to taste and allow to simmer gently for 2 minutes. Pour into individual serving bowls and garnish with chopped spring onion.

Dobin Mushi *(kettle soup)*

4 dried Japanese mushrooms
50 g ginkgo nuts
75 g fresh shrimps
75 g white chicken meat
75 g white fish fillet
1 litre dashi
2 teaspoons Japanese soya sauce
2 teaspoons sake
salt to taste

Soak the mushrooms in cold water for 2 hours, then trim and cut into small pieces. Simmer the ginkgo nuts until tender, then drain and remove skins. Shell and de-vein the shrimps and carefully remove any skin from the chicken and fish. Chop the shrimp, chicken and fish into small pieces, combine with the mushroom and ginkgo nuts and place in a saucepan. Add just sufficient cold water to cover and bring to the boil. Immediately lower heat and simmer for approximately 15 minutes, then pour away the water and add the dashi. Bring back to the boil, add soya sauce, sake and salt to taste and simmer for 1 minute before pouring into small individual 'kettles'.
The tops of these special 'kettles' are tiny bowls and the soup should be poured into these while the solid foods are removed and eaten with chopsticks.

Suimono *(clear soup)*

2 pieces wakame (dried seaweed)
75 g bamboo shoot
2 leaves Chinese cabbage
1 litre dashi
25 ml Japanese soya sauce
salt to taste
pinch monosodium glutamate
1 spring onion, chopped

Soak the seaweed in cold water for approximately 20 minutes. Cut the seaweed, bamboo shoot and cabbage into small pieces and sprinkle a little soya sauce on top. In a saucepan, bring the dashi to a rapid boil, add the salt, monosodium glutamate and remaining soya sauce and stir to blend thoroughly. Lower heat, add bamboo shoot and cabbage and allow to simmer for 5–6 minutes. Place a little seaweed in the bottom of individual serving bowls, pour in the soup and garnish with chopped spring onion.

Zousui *(rice soup)*

100 g long grain rice
1 litre dashi
2 spring onions
2 young spinach leaves
2 teaspoons Japanese soya sauce
salt to taste
pinch monosodium glutamate
2 eggs
1 teaspoon chopped watercress

Boil the rice until tender, then place in cold water and break-up with a fork before straining thoroughly. In a saucepan, bring the dashi to the boil and add the rice. Chop the spring onions and add to the stock together with the spinach leaves. Season with soya sauce, salt and monosodium glutamate, lower heat and simmer for 7–8 minutes. Break the eggs into a bowl and beat lightly with a fork. Add to the stock and bring back to a boil, stirring continuously until the egg begins to set. Serve immediately into individual bowls and garnish with chopped watercress.

Hamaguri Ushiojiru *(clam soup)*

20 clams
2 spring onions
peel of $\frac{1}{2}$ lemon
1 litre water
25 ml Japanese soya sauce
25 ml mirin
$\frac{1}{2}$ teaspoon salt
pinch monosodium glutamate

Wash the clams in salt water and scrub with a stiff brush to clean thoroughly. Chop the spring onions and cut the lemon peel into thin strips. In a saucepan, bring the water to a rapid boil and add the clams. After 1 minute, lower heat and simmer until all the clams open, discarding any that fail to do so. Add the onion, soya sauce, mirin, salt and monosodium glutamate and allow to simmer for a further 5 minutes. Finally add the chopped lemon peel, stir well and transfer to individual soup bowls.

Kakejiru *(grilled eels)*

4 small eels
50 ml oil
750 ml kake-tare sauce
600 g cooked rice

Kake-tare sauce:
400 ml mirin
400 ml Japanese soya sauce
100 g brown sugar

Cut off the heads and tails from the eels, slit along the underside and remove the backbone. Clean thoroughly and spread out on a flat surface. Cut the eels in half, crosswise, and skewer each piece with 4 evenly-spaced skewers, taking care not to pierce the meat on either side. Brush with the oil and cook under a fairly hot grill for 15 minutes; the skin-side for 10 minutes and the underside for 5 minutes. Remove from the grill and brush with the prepared kare-take sauce, then return to grill and cook for a further 2–3 minutes. Repeat this process a few times until the eel is cooked and well-glazed, then remove the skewers carefully, taking care not to tear the meat. To serve; place a bed of steaming-hot cooked rice into four serving bowls, arrange 2 pieces of eels on top of each and pour the remaining sauce over the eel.

To prepare the sauce, combine all the ingredients in a saucepan and bring to a rapid boil. Lower heat and allow to simmer, stirring frequently, until the sugar has dissolved and the mixture attains a smooth, syrupy consistency. Then, remove from heat and, using a wooden ladle, agitate in an up-and-down movement for about 10 minutes.

Unagi Unatama *(eel with egg)*

4 small eels
50 ml oil
500 ml kare-tare sauce
  (see recipe above)
800 g cooked rice
650 ml cold water
25 ml sake
2 teaspoons sugar
pinch monosodium glutamate
2 eggs

Prepare and cook the eels as described in recipe above, using approximately half the kake-tare for glazing. Arrange the eels on four beds of cooked rice. Pour the remaining sauce into a pan, add the water, sake, sugar and monosodium glutamate and bring to a rapid boil, stirring continuously. Break the eggs into the sauce and whisk with a fork until the egg begins to set. Pour the sauce over the eel and serve immediately.

UNAGI (eels) photographed at **Miyagawa Restaurant,** Tokyo (see next page)

Chawan Mushi *(seafood in egg custard)*

100 g fresh shrimps
100 g white fish fillet
50 g white chicken meat
50 g green beans
1 spring onion
850 ml dashi (recipe page 7)
25 ml Japanese soya sauce
25 ml mirin
salt to taste
pinch monosodium glutamate
4 eggs

Shell and de-vein the shrimps and make sure all the skin and bones are removed from the fish and chicken meat. Cut the shrimps in half lengthwise, flake the fish and cut the chicken into small dice. Place in a pan, cover with water and cook until tender. Strain and transfer to heat-proof bowls. Slice the beans, cook until tender and place into the bowls. Pour the dashi into a saucepan, add the soya sauce, mirin, salt and monosodium glutamate and bring to the boil. Lower heat and allow to simmer for 2–3 minutes, then remove from the heat and allow to cool. Next, break the eggs into the stock and stir thoroughly, then pour into the individual bowls and cover the bowls with tightly-fitting lids or foil. Place the bowls into a large shallow pan of boiling water (the water should come half-way to the top of the bowls) and steam until the egg sets. Serve immediately.

Ebigohan *(shrimps with rice)*

150 g fresh shrimps
2 cloves garlic
1 small brown onion
2 small carrots
2 spring onions
25 ml vegetable oil
25 g butter
4 eggs
150 g cooked rice
25 ml Japanese soya sauce
freshly ground black pepper
salt to taste
pinch monosodium glutamate

Shell and de-vein the shrimps and cut into small pieces. Crush the garlic and finely chop the onion, carrots and spring onion. Heat the oil in a shallow pan and sauté the garlic until golden and crispy. Add the butter and allow to melt, then add the shrimps and cook for 2–3 minutes, stirring continuously. Next add the vegetables, stir to blend thoroughly and continue to cook for a further 2 minutes. Break the eggs into the mixture, stir well and cook until the egg begins to set. Finally add the rice, soya sauce, freshly ground black pepper, salt and monosodium glutamate. Blend throughly, allow the rice time to heat through, then serve immediately.

Kuroke *(fish croquettes)*

600 g white fish fillets
4 small carrots
3 spring onions
1 egg
25 g cornstarch
salt to taste
oil for deep frying
Sauce:
50 ml Japanese soya sauce
25 ml tomato ketchup
2 teaspoons mirin
1 teaspoon hot mustard

Remove the skin from the fish and check carefully to make sure no small bones remain. Chop the fish into tiny pieces and place in a mixing bowl. Shred the carrots and finely chop the spring onion and add to the fish. Add the egg, cornstarch and salt to taste and stir to blend thoroughly. Mould the mixture into small patties, adding a little more cornstarch if necessary. Heat the oil to 200°C (400°F) and deep-fry the patties until cooked and golden brown. Serve with a side-dish of sauce for dipping.

To make the sauce, blend together all the ingredients in a pan and bring to a low bowl. Remove from heat and allow to cool before serving.

Yosenabe *(seafood with vegetables)*

2 lobster tails
300 g red snapper fillets
300 g halibut fillets
150 g cuttlefish
6 oysters
6 clams
100 g transparent noodles
1 square kombu (seaweed)
½ small Chinese cabbage
2 carrots
4 spring onions
800 ml dashi (recipe page 7)
6 mushrooms
25 ml Japanese soya sauce
25 ml mirin

Clean and prepare all the seafood and cut into bite-size pieces. Soak the noodles in cold water until soft then cut into short lengths. Soak the seaweed in cold water for 15 minutes. Shred the cabbage and slice the carrots. Cut the spring onions into 25 cm lengths. Place a cooking pot in the centre of the table, pour in the dashi and bring to the boil. Add the seaweed and noodles and simmer for 3–4 minutes then add the cabbage, carrots and mushrooms and continue to cook for a further 2 minutes. Add the soya sauce and mirin, stir to blend thoroughly, then add all the seafood and allow to simmer until cooked, making sure all the clams have opened. Finally add the spring onion and stir well. Transfer to individual bowls and serve immediately.

Stuffed Red Snappers

4 small red snappers
100 ml sake
1 teaspoon salt
150 g tofu (bean curd)
1 carrot
3 mushrooms
2 spring onion
125 ml dashi (recipe page 7)
25 ml Japanese soya sauce
2 teaspoons sugar
salt to taste
freshly ground white pepper
2 eggs

For basting:
50 ml Japanese soya sauce
50 ml mirin
2 teaspoons sugar

Cut the fish along the dorsal fins and remove bones. Clean thoroughly and rub the sake and salt into the cavities of the fish. Chop the bean curd and vegetables into small pieces and place into a saucepan. Add the dashi, soya sauce, sugar and salt and bring to the boil. Lower heat and simmer until the vegetables are cooked, then beat the eggs lightly and add to the mixture. Continue to cook over a low heat, stirring continuously, until the mixture begins to thicken. Remove from heat and allow to cool then stuff the mixture into the cavities of the fish. Place fish into a pre-heated moderately-hot oven and bake for 8–10 minutes, basting occasionally with a mixture of the soya sauce, mirin and sugar.

STUFFED RED SNAPPERS photographed at **The Genji,** Tokyo Hilton

KANI-KORAAGE (opposite) photographed at **Kani Seryna Restaurant,** Tokyo

Kani-Koraage *(deep fried stuffed crabs)*

4 medium-size crabs
2 teaspoons vinegar
$\frac{1}{2}$ teaspoon salt
150 g fresh shrimps
4 Japanese mushrooms
100 g ginkgo nuts
50 g bamboo shoot
2 cloves garlic
2 spring onions
oil for cooking
salt to taste
freshly ground white pepper
25 ml sake
1 egg
25 g cornstarch
25 g breadcrumbs

Sauce:
100 ml Japanese soya sauce
25 ml mirin
25 g sugar
50 ml mayonnaise
50 ml tomato ketchup
freshly ground white pepper

Place the crabs into a bowl of rapidly-boiling water, add the vinegar and salt and cook until tender. Remove the back shells carefully, clean throughly in salt water and set these aside. Extract all the meat from the body and claws. Shell and de-vein the shrimps. Soak the mushrooms in cold water until soft then trim and chop into small pieces. Boil the ginkgo nuts until tender and remove skins. Cut the bamboo shoot into small dice, crush the garlic and cut the spring onion into 25 cm lengths. Heat 50 ml of the oil in a pan and sauté the garlic for 2–3 minutes then add the shrimp and all the other vegetables, season with salt and white pepper and cook for a further 3–4 minutes, stirring frequently. Flake the crabmeat and add to the mixture together with the sake. Beat the egg lightly and mix with the cornstarch then add this to the crab mixture in the pan and stir to blend thoroughly. Dust the inside of the crab shells with a little flour then spoon the mixture into the shells and sprinkle breadcrumbs on top. In a large pan, heat the remaining oil to 200°C (400°F) and deep-fry the stuffed shells until the tops are a golden brown colour. Remove from the oil, drain thoroughly and serve with side dishes of sauce.

To make the sauce, pour the soya sauce and mirin into a small saucepan and add the sugar. Bring to the boil and stir until the sugar has completely dissolved. Add all the remaining ingredients, stir to blend thoroughly and remove from the heat. Allow to cool before serving.

Tempura

12 medium-size prawns
400 g fish fillets
8 fresh mushrooms
2 small brown onions
4 spring onions
1 small eggplant
4 asparagus spears
small can bamboo shoot
small can ginkgo nuts
oil for deep frying

Batter:
1 egg
300 ml ice-cold water
pinch baking soda
200 g all-purpose flour

Tempura sauce:
75 ml mirin
75 ml Japanese soya sauce
150 ml dashi (recipe page 7)
$\frac{1}{4}$ teaspoon salt
pinch monosodium glutamate
25 g grated radish

Shell and de-vein the prawns but leave the tails intact. Remove any skin from the fish and ensure that no small bones remain then cut into bite-size pieces. Cut all the vegetables into bite-size pieces and place 3 or 4 ginkgo nuts on wooden skewers. To cook: dip the pieces of food into the prepared batter and deep-fry in the oil. (Note: It is important that the oil be kept at an even temperature, approximately 190°C (375°F) during the whole period of cooking. Only a few pieces should be cooked at a time and the oil continually brought back to the desired temperature. While cooking, the food should be turned occasionally with long wooden chopsticks and, when cooked, should be placed on sheets of absorbent paper arranged on serving plates.) Serve with a side-dish of Tempura sauce.

To make the batter, break the egg into a mixing bowl and add the ice-cold water. Add the baking soda and flour and mix thoroughly until the batter is perfectly smooth and thin. If the batter appears too thick add a little more ice-cold water. (Note: It is important that the batter be of the correct consistency and must be freshly made just prior to using. It should never be stored, even for a short period.)

To make the sauce, heat the mirin in a small saucepan until it is warm (but not too hot), then remove from the heat and light with a match. Shake the pan slightly until the flame dies then add the soya sauce and dashi, return to the heat and bring to the boil. Season with salt and monosodium glutamate and allow to cool. Finally, add the grated radish and stir to blend thoroughly.

TEMPURA photographed at **The Genji,** Tokyo Hilton

Sashimi & Sushi

To many, these famous raw fish preparations provide the most exotic tastes to be found in Japanese cuisine. For here, only the choisest and freshest of fish is ever used; often taken from a fish tank just prior to preparation, to ensure an absolute perfection of flavour so vital to this culinary masterpiece.

The fish must be carefully skinned, boned and cleaned; rinsed in boiling water to eliminate the possibility of any surface bacteria, then immersed immediately in cold water. The fish is carefully sliced into sections measuring about 6 cm × 4 cm × 8 mm (the size, naturally, may vary depending on the kind of fish used). The most commonly used fish include tuna, sea bass, bream and sole, while octupus, squid and prawn, also very popular, all add their own unique texture and flavour.

Sashimi is usually served on individual dishes with a garnish of watercress or parsley and a dish of dipping sauce which may consist of soya sauce mixed with grated horseradish or a variety of other ingredients, such as lemon juice, grated ginger or hot mustard, according to taste.

For Sushi, small portions of vinegared rice are formed by hand into oblong shapes. Horseradish is added and a piece of fish placed on top. A very popular variation is to spread a layer of rice on top of a sheet of kombu (seaweed), place a pickle, vegetable or some horseradish in the centre, roll up and cut into slices.

Sushi Rice

500 g rice
50 ml rice vinegar
50 ml mirin
75 g sugar
$\frac{1}{2}$ teaspoon salt
pinch monosodium glutamate

Place the rice in a saucepan, cover with water and cook until ready. Keep the pan covered and remove from the heat. In a fresh saucepan, combine the vinegar, mirin, sugar, salt and monosodium glutamate and bring to the boil. Immediately lower heat and allow to simmer, uncovered, for 7–8 minutes, then pour on to the cooked rice and mix thoroughly with a fork. Replace the cover on the pan and allow to cool before using.

GRILLED TROUT photographed at **The Genji,** Tokyo Hilton

Teppanyaki Ise-Ebi *(lobster teppanyaki)*

850 g fresh lobster meat
2 large green peppers
1 large brown onion
75 g butter
25 ml fresh lemon juice
25 ml fresh lemon juice
½ teaspoon salt
freshly ground white pepper
50 ml mirin

Sauce:
1 small brown onion
1 clove garlic
25 mm knob fresh ginger
25 ml vegetable oil
25 ml Japanese soya sauce
25 ml tomato sauce
25 ml Worcestershire sauce
25 ml fresh lemon juice
100 ml dashi (recipe page 7)
2 teaspoons cornstarch

Cut the lobster meat into bite-size chunks and chop the green peppers and onion. Melt half the butter on a large open griddle, add the lobster and cook for 2 minutes, turning frequently. Melt the remaining butter apart from the lobster and fry the pepper and onion for 2–3 minutes, while the lobster continues to cook separately. Then bring all the food together, add the soya sauce and lemon juice and season with salt and freshly ground white pepper. Mix thoroughly and continue to cook until the lobster meat is tender (the vegetables should still be crispy), then add the mirin, toss well and serve on to individual plates. Serve with side-dishes of the prepared sauce.

To make the sauce: chop the onion, garlic and ginger very finely. Heat the oil in a saucepan, add the chopped vegetables and sauté for 3–4 minutes Add the soya sauce, tomato sauce, Worcestershire sauce, lemon juice and dashi and bring to the boil, then immediately lower heat and simmer for 5 minutes. Mix the cornstarch with a small quantity of cold water and stir into the sauce to thicken slightly. Allow to cool before serving.

Gyruniku Teppanyaki *(beef teppanyaki)*

750 g prime beef steak
100 ml mirin
100 ml Japanese soya sauce
freshly ground black pepper
8 cloves garlic
150 g bean sprouts
oil for frying

Sauce:
50 g white radish
25 mm knob fresh ginger
50 ml mirin
75 ml Japanese soya sauce
2 teaspoons sugar

Cut the beef into bite-size pieces and place in a shallow dish. Pour half the mirin and soya sauce over the beef, season with freshly ground black pepper and set aside for 30 minutes. Chop the garlic finely and trim the ends of the bean sprouts. Pour a little oil on to a large open griddle and fry the garlic until it is golden and crispy, then push to one side. Add a little more oil and fry the beef for 4–5 minutes, turning occasionally and adding a little of the remaining mirin and soya sauce during the cooking period. When the meat is almost cooked, pour more oil on to the griddle and cook the bean sprouts (separately to the meat) using the remaining mirin and soya sauce and tossing well for 2 minutes.

To serve: place portions of beef, bean sprouts and garlic on a plate in front of each diner and serve the sauce in a side-dish.

To make the sauce: grate the radish and ginger and mix with the mirin and soya sauce. Add the sugar and stir until completely dissolved.

23

Buta-no-Shoga-Yaki *(ginger fried pork)*

500 g lean pork tenderloin
2 cloves garlic
2 spring onions
30 mm knob fresh ginger
125 ml Japanese soya sauce
25 ml mirin
pinch monosodium glutamate
oil for frying

Chill the pork slightly so that it may be cut into very thin slices. Chop the garlic, spring onions and half the ginger and combine with the soya sauce, mirin and monosodium glutamate. Cut the remaining ginger into very thin slices. Place a layer of pork slices in a shallow dish and pour a little of the soya sauce mixture on top. Repeat until all the pork has been arranged in the dish, then place in the refrigerator and allow to marinate for 45 minutes. To cook; heat the oil in a shallow frying pan, add the slices of ginger and cook for 2 minutes. Then add the pork, removing directly from the dish so that a little of the marinade is also included, and cook over a high heat, turning once, until both sides are golden brown. Serve immediately with shredded red cabbage.

Tonkatsu *(breaded pork fillets)*

4 pork fillets
$\frac{1}{4}$ teaspoon salt
$\frac{1}{4}$ teaspoon white pepper
$\frac{1}{4}$ teaspoon garlic powder
2 eggs
150 g white breadcrumbs
oil for frying
15 mm knob fresh ginger
1 teaspoon freshly chopped parsley

Pound the fillets to make thin, then season with salt, white pepper and garlic powder and place into a shallow dish. Beat the eggs and pour over the pork and set aside for 10–15 minutes. Remove the pork from the egg and coat thoroughly with the breadcrumbs. Heat the oil in a shallow frying pan and cook the pork, turning once, until golden brown. Remove from the pan and drain thoroughly, then cut the pork, crosswise, into slices. Transfer to a serving plate and arrange in the original fillet shapes. Finally, grate the ginger and sprinkle on top of the meat and garnish with freshly chopped parsley.

ISIYAKI (opposite page) is a meal of prime Japanese beef, cooked at the tableside on a pre-heated hot rock, and served with fresh vegetables.

SHABU-SHABU photographed at **Seryna Restaurant,** Tokyo

Shabu-Shabu *(beef steamboat)*

650 g lean beef steak
small Chinese cabbage
6 small carrots
75 g spinach leaves
4 large fresh mushrooms
200 g tofu (bean curd)
6 spring onions
1.2 litres chicken stock

Sesame seed dip:
1 shallot
2 anchovy fillets
50 g roasted sesame seeds
25 g roasted cashew nuts
50 ml vinegar
50 ml Japanese soya sauce
2 teaspoons sugar
½ teaspoon salt

Freeze the beef slightly so that it may be cut into very thin slices. Discard the stem and outer leaves from the cabbage and slice the carrots lengthwise. Parboil the cabbage, carrots and spinach separately and drain well. Slice the mushrooms and bean curd and cut the spring onions into 25 mm lengths. Arrange the cabbage and spinach leaves on a large plate, place the sliced beef on top and surround with the remaining vegetables and bean curd. Place a shabu-shabu cooker (or steamboat) in the middle of the table and fill the chimmney with hot charcoal. Bring the stock to a rapid boil and pour into the cooker. (The stock should remain simmering while each diner selects from the serving plate and cooks his own food.) Serve with a prepared sesame seed dip.

To make the dip: chop the shallot and anchovy very finely and grind together with the roasted sesame seeds and cashew nuts. Add the vinegar, soya sauce, sugar and salt and blend thoroughly to form a thick, smooth dip.

26

Sukiyaki *(sliced beef & vegetables)*

600 g prime beef steak
1 large brown onion
6 large fresh mushrooms
200 g tofu (bean curd)
150 g canned bamboo shoot
6 spring onions
small Chinese cabbage
150 g bean sprouts
100 g transparent noodles
1 piece beef fat
3 teaspoons sugar
100 ml sake
200 ml Japanese soya sauce
4 fresh eggs (for dipping)

Freeze the beef slightly so that it may be cut into very thin slices. Slice the brown onion, mushrooms, bean curd and bamboo shoot. Cut the cabbage into bite size pieces and cut the spring onions into 25 mm lengths. Wash the bean sprouts, trim the ends and blanch for 1 minute. Cook the noodles and cut into short lengths. Arrange all the ingredients on plates and place on the table. Pre-heat an iron pan over a flame in the centre of the table and grease well with the beef fat. Place a few slices of meat into the pan and cook for 2 minutes, turning once. Sprinkle the sugar over the meat and add a selection of vegetables. Cook for a further minute, stirring continuously, then pour in the sake and half the soya sauce and add the bean curd and noodles. Allow each diner to serve himself with chopsticks directly from the pan and cook the remaining meat and vegetables as required, adding the rest of the soya sauce a little at a time. The eggs should be broken into small individual side-bowls, lightly beaten with the chopsticks and used as a dip for the beef.

SUKIYAKI photographed at **The Genji,** Tokyo Hilton

Sunomono *(vegetable salad)*

1 small cucumber
½ small Chinese cabbage
75 g white radish
50 ml rice vinegar
100 ml dashi (recipe page 7)
50 ml Japanese soya sauce
25 ml mirin
2 teaspoons fresh lemon juice
2 teaspoons sugar
1 egg-yolk
salt to taste
freshly ground black pepper

Wash the vegetables and dry thoroughly. Slice the cucumber and shred the cabbage and radish and place into a bowl. Combine the vinegar, dashi, mirin and lemon juice in a saucepan and bring to the boil. Lower heat, add the sugar and allow to simmer for 3–4 minutes. Whisk the egg-yolk lightly, then add to the simmering stock. Season to taste with salt and freshly ground black pepper and continue to cook over a low heat, stirring frequently, until the sauce thickens. Remove from heat and allow to cool before pouring over the vegetables. Allow to stand for 30 minutes, then serve into individual bowls.

Yaki-Nasu *(baked eggplant)*

2 eggplants
½ teaspoon salt
¼ teaspoon white pepper
50 ml vegetable oil
2 teaspoons bonito flakes
20 mm knob fresh ginger
100 ml Japanese soya sauce
25 ml mirin

Wash the eggplants under cold running water, dry thoroughly and cut into halves, lengthways. Do not remove the skin. Season with salt and freshly ground white pepper and allow to stand for 20–25 minutes. Then brush the eggplant with oil, place under a hot grill and cook until tender. Slice the eggplant, arrange pieces on a serving plate and sprinkle the bonito flakes on top. Cut the ginger into very fine shreds, mix with the soya sauce and mirin and serve as a dip.

Matsutake Tsutsumi-Yaki *(grilled mushrooms)*

12 large dried Japanese mushrooms
2 teaspoons light soya sauce
50 ml Japanese soya sauce
50 ml mirin
2 teaspoons fresh lemon juice
25 g sugar
salt to taste
freshly ground white pepper
¼ teaspoon monosodium glutamate
25 g cornstarch

Wash the mushrooms under cold running water, then place into a pan and cover with cold water. Allow the mushrooms to soak for 1 hour, then remove from the water, dry thoroughly and discard the hard stems. Sprinkle a little light soya sauce over the mushrooms and securely wrap individually in foil. Place under a hot grill and cook until tender. In the meantime bring the water the mushrooms soaked in to the boil, add the Japanese soya sauce, mirin, lemon juice, sugar, salt, pepper and monosodium glutamate and stir to blend thoroughly. Bring back to the boil, lower heat and allow to simmer for 2–3 minutes. Mix the cornstarch with a small quantity of cold water and add to the sauce to thicken slightly. To serve; remove the foil from the mushrooms, arrange on a serving plate and pour the sauce on top.

Kabu-no-Tsukemono *(pickled radish)*

4 medium size white turnips
1 teaspoon salt
100 ml vinegar
25 ml mirin
25 g sugar
red food colouring

Wash the turnips under cold running water. Dry thoroughly, then cut into very thin slices, sprinkle the salt on top and set aside for 30 minutes. Press the radish in a clean cloth to squeeze out any excess moisture, then place into a large bowl. Combine the vinegar, mirin and sugar and stir until the sugar has completely dissolved. Pour the mixture over the radish and add a few drops of red colouring. Allow to stand for 1 hour before transferring to individual salad bowls.

Note: The amount of food colouring is a matter of preference. Usually the aim is to turn the radish to a deep pink.

Horenso-no-Goma-ae *(sesame spinach)*

400 g spinach
1 teaspoon salt
freshly ground white pepper
50 g sesame seeds
75 ml Japanese soya sauce
2 teaspoons sake
2 teaspoons sugar

Wash the spinach thoroughly under cold running water, trim and tie into a bunch with the stems together. Bring a large pan of water to the boil, add salt and cook the spinach until tender. Remove the spinach and drain well, then cut into pieces and arrange on a serving plate. Season with freshly ground white pepper and additional salt, if required. In the meantime, dry-fry the sesame seeds until they start to pop, then remove and place through a grinder. Mix the ground sesame seed with the soya sauce, sake and sugar, stir to blend thoroughly, then pour over the spinach.

Nimono *(mixed braised vegetables)*

150 g bamboo shoot
100 g yam
100 g turnip
1 long white radish
6 carrots
2 brown onions
6 fresh mushrooms
1 litre dashi (recipe page 7)
100 ml mirin
25 ml Japanese soya sauce
salt to taste
25 g cornstarch (optional)

Prepare all the vegetables, cutting into appropriate serving size pieces, then par-boil each separately. Drain all the vegetables and arrange in a large pan. Add the dashi, mirin, soya sauce and bring to the boil. Immediately lower heat, cover the pan and cook slowly for approximately 20 minutes. Drain the vegetables thoroughly and arrange on a serving plate. If a sauce is desired, pour 75 ml of the cooking stock into a small saucepan and bring to the boil. Mix the cornstarch with a small quantity of cold water, add to the stock and allow to simmer, stirring frequently, until the sauce thickens, then pour over the vegetables.

NIMONO (recipe page 29)

Oyako Domburi *(chicken & egg domburi)*

350 g white chicken meat
3 spring onions
600 ml dashi
125 ml Japanese soya sauce
125 ml mirin
25 ml sake
25 g sugar
6 eggs
salt to taste
freshly ground white pepper
pinch monosodium glutamate
750 g cooked rice
1 sheet nori (seaweed)

Remove any skin from the chicken meat and cut into small cubes of approximately 12 mm. Cut the spring onions into thin slices. Pour the dashi into a saucepan, add the soya sauce, mirin, sake and sugar and bring to the boil. Add the pieces of chicken, lower heat, cover the pan and allow to simmer for 7–8 minutes. Then remove cover, add the spring onion and continue to cook slowly for a further minute. Break the eggs into a mixing bowl, add salt, freshly ground white pepper and monosodium glutamate and beat lightly. Add the egg to the simmering stock and bring back to a rapid boil. Immediately lower heat, cover the pan and cook slowly until the egg begins to set (the egg should remain soft), approximately 3–4 minutes. To serve; place portions of steaming-hot rice into individual serving bowls and, with a ladle, add the chicken and egg stock. Crumble the seaweed and sprinkle on top as a garnish.

OYAKO DONBURI photographed at **Seryna Restaurant,** Tokyo

Toriniku-no-Sumashi *(chicken balls in soup)*

400 g white chicken meat
20 mm knob fresh ginger
4 spring onions
50 g cornstarch
1 egg white
50 ml Japanese soya sauce
25 ml sake
salt to taste
freshly ground white pepper
1 litre dashi (recipe page 7)
$\frac{1}{4}$ small Chinese cabbage
$\frac{1}{4}$ teaspoon chopped lemon peel

Remove any skin from the chicken and cut into small pieces. Chop the ginger and 2 of the spring onions, mix with the chicken and place through a coarse mincer. Combine with the cornstarch, egg-white, sake and half the soya sauce and shape into small balls. Place in a covered steamer and cook over rapidly boiling water for approximately 10 minutes. In the meantime, pour the dashi into a saucepan and bring to the boil. Add the cabbage and remaining soya sauce and allow to simmer for 5 minutes. Chop the remaining spring onions and add to the simmering stock together with the chicken balls. Adjust seasonings to taste, stir well for a further minute, then transfer to individual bowls and sprinkle a little chopped lemon peel on top.

Tori Teriyaki *(chicken teriyaki)*

4 chicken breasts
2 cloves garlic
2 cloves garlic
20 mm knob fresh ginger
100 ml dashi
50 ml mirin
50 ml Japanese soya sauce
25 g sugar
oil for frying
25 g cornstarch
2 teaspoons brown sugar

Bone the chicken breasts, score the skin with a sharp knife and place into a shallow dish. Chop the garlic and ginger very finely. Combine the dashi, mirin and soya sauce and add the garlic, ginger and sugar. Stir to blend thoroughly, then pour the mixture over the chicken and set aside for 30–40 minutes, turning the chicken pieces occasionally during marination. Remove chicken and pat dry. Heat the oil in a frying pan until it starts to smoke, then brown the chicken quickly on both sides. Add half the reserved marinade and bring to the boil, then immediately lower heat, cover the pan and cook slowly until the chicken is tender. Remove and arrange the chicken on a serving plate (leave the breasts whole or slice, as preferred). Pour the remaining reserved marinade into a small saucepan, add a small quantity of cold water, the cornstarch and brown sugar and bring to a boil. Lower heat and simmer for 3–4 minutes, stirring continuously, until the sauce thickens, then pour over the chicken and serve immediately.

Note: If preferred, the chicken can be cooked under a grill or broiler. In this case the chicken should be placed under the grill immediately it is removed from the marinade and should be brushed with the reserved marinade frequently during the period of cooking.

Torimaki *(chicken omelette)*

200 g cooked chicken meat
15 mm knob fresh ginger
2 teaspoons sugar
25 ml mirin
50 ml Japanese soya sauce
6 eggs
50 ml dashi (recipe page 7)
salt to taste
freshly ground white pepper
oil for cooking

Remove any skin from the chicken and cut into very small dice. Chop the ginger very finely and combine with the chicken. Add the sugar, mirin and half the soya sauce, mix thoroughly and set aside. Break the eggs into a mixing bowl, add the dashi, salt, freshly ground white pepper and remaining soya sauce and beat lightly. Heat an omelette pan and add a small quantity of oil. Pour in half the egg mixture and cook until the bottom is set but the top is still soft. Place half the chicken filling across the centre and roll the omelette around the filling. Cook for a further 2–3 minutes, turning ocassionally to ensure an even golden colour. Repeat with the remaining mixtures and serve immediately or allow to stand, slice and serve cold.

Tori-no-Koraage *(deep fried chicken)*

1 fresh chicken, about 1 kilo
2 cloves garlic
25 mm knob fresh ginger
2 spring onions
125 ml Japanese soya sauce
50 ml mirin
25 ml sake
100 g cornstarch
$\frac{1}{2}$ teaspoon salt
freshly ground white pepper
pinch monosodium glutamate
oil for deep frying
25 g crispy fried chopped onion

Clean and prepare the chicken and cut into eight pieces. Chop the garlic, ginger and spring onions. Combine the soya sauce, mirin and sake in a saucepan, add the garlic, ginger and spring onion and bring to the boil. Lower heat and simmer for 2 minutes, then pour over the chicken and set aside to marinate for approximately 45 minutes. Remove the chicken from the marinade and drain thoroughly. Mix the cornstarch with salt, freshly ground white pepper and monosodium glutamate and use to coat the chicken. Heat the oil in a fairly deep pan until it reaches approximately 180°C (350°F) and deep-fry the chicken until cooked and golden brown. Remove from the oil, drain well and arrange on a serving plate. Sprinkle the crispy fried onion pieces on top.

Goma-Yaki *(sesame chicken)*

4 chicken breasts
$\frac{1}{2}$ teaspoon salt
$\frac{1}{4}$ teaspoon white pepper
100 ml mirin
25 ml sake
25 ml Japanese soya sauce
25 g sesame seeds
1 clove garlic
oil for shallow frying
4 lettuce leaves

Bone the chicken breasts, prick the skin with a fork and place into a shallow dish. Rub salt and pepper into the skin of the chicken. Combine the mirin, sake and soya sauce, pour over the chicken and set aside for 45 minutes. Dry-fry the sesame seeds until they start to pop, then remove and set aside to cool. Crush the garlic. Heat the oil in a frying pan, add the garlic and sauté for 3–4 minutes, then add the chicken breasts and, over a high heat, brown both sides. Lower heat and cook until the chicken is tender, then remove, cut into slices and arrange on lettuce leaves. Sprinkle the sesame seeds on top and serve immediately.

Yakitori

Yakitori bars are to be found all over Japan offering a variety of combinations of chicken and vegetables, threaded on skewers and cooked over hot charcoal. Chicken wings with spring onions, chicken livers with ginger and mushrooms and minced chicken balls with shiso leaves are but three popular combinations. When preparing at home it's a matter of personal preference using, in addition to the above: white chicken meat, chicken gizzards and skin, asparagus, green peppers and eggplant. To prepare: make the marinade (see recipe below), pour over the chicken and set aside for 1 hour. Place a few pieces of chosen food on to a skewer, alternating the chicken and vegetables (each skewer should not hold more than six pieces, the idea being to serve a large variety of sticks). Mix the reserved marinade with a similar quantity of dashi and use the mixture to brush the food while cooking.

Yakitori Marinade

2 shallots
3 cloves garlic
25 mm knob fresh ginger
125 ml Japanese soya sauce
125 ml mirin
25 ml golden honey
25 g soft brown sugar
freshly ground black pepper
200 ml dashi (recipe page 7)

Chop the shallots, garlic and ginger very finely and pound together to produce a smooth paste. Pour the soya sauce and mirin into a saucepan and bring almost to the boil. Add the pounded vegetables, honey, sugar and freshly ground black pepper and stir to blend thoroughly. Simmer over a low heat (do not allow to come to a rapid boil) until the honey and sugar have completely dissolved. Allow to cool before pouring over the pieces of chicken. After the chicken has been removed, add the dashi to the marinade, blend well and use to baste during cooking.

YAKITORI photographed **Kushihachi Restaurant,** Tokyo

35

Kitsune Domburi *(rice with fried bean curd)*

4 sheets auberge (fried bean curd)
650 ml dashi (recipe page 7)
125 ml Japanese soya sauce
125 ml mirin
25 ml sugar
¼ teaspoon salt
450 g cooked rice

If the auberge is frozen allow time to completely thaw out then, rinse thoroughly under hot water, drain and cut into narrow strips. Place the auberge into a saucepan, add the dashi, soya sauce and mirin and bring to the boil. Lower heat, add the sugar and salt and allow to simmer for 10 minutes, stirring occasionally. Slice the spring onions finely, add to the stock and continue to cook slowly for a further 2 minutes. To serve: place portions of rice into individual serving bowls and pour the hot soup on top.

Summertime Tofu

8 squares tofu (bean curd)
½ teaspoon salt
20 mm knob fresh ginger
1 spring onion
pinch monosodium glutamate
150 ml Japanese soya sauce

Place the tofu in a large saucepan, cover with water, add the salt and bring slowly to the boil. Lower heat and allow to simmer gently for 10 minutes, then remove from the pan and allow to cool. Cut the tofu into bite-size pieces and transfer to a serving bowl containing iced water. Serve a dip in individual side dishes. To make the dip first grate the ginger and place a small mound in the centre of each dish. Then chop the spring onion very finely and place around the ginger. Finally, add the monosodium glutamate and soya sauce and mix well with chopsticks.

Wintertime Tofu

8 squares tofu (bean curd)
small square kombu (dried seaweed)
½ teaspoon salt
50 g dried bonito flakes
1 spring onion
125 ml Japanese soya sauce
25 ml sake
pinch monosodium glutamate
freshly ground white pepper

Place the tofu in a large saucepan and cover with cold water. Cut the kombu into strips and add to the pan. Bring slowly to the boil, add the salt and allow to simmer for 5 minutes. Then, add the bonito flakes and continue to cook slowly for a further 5 minutes. Cut the tofu into bite-size pieces and transfer to an earthenware pot in the centre of the table. Bring the stock back to the boil and pour over the tofu. Serve the dip in individual side dishes. To make the dip; chop the spring onion very finely and place a little in each side dish. Add a small quantity of the cooking stock together with an equal amount of soya sauce and a dash of sake. Season with monosodium glutamate and freshly ground white pepper and mix thoroughly with chopsticks.

Kabayaki *(basic soba stock)*

1 litre dashi
100 ml Japanese soya sauce
100 ml mirin
½ teaspoon salt
pinch monosodium glutamate

Pour the dashi into a saucepan and bring to the boil. Add the soya sauce, mirin, salt and monosodium glutamate and stir to blend thoroughly. Cover the pan and allow to simmer for 10–12 minutes.

Tempura Soba

400 g buckwheat noodles
4 large prawns
4 small fillets white fish
tempura batter (recipe page 16)
oil for cooking
1 litre kakejiru stock (see above)
salt to taste
freshly ground white pepper
2 spring onions

Cook the noodles and drain thoroughly. Shell and de-vein the prawns, leaving the tails intact. Remove any skin from the fish and make certain no bones remain. Coat the prawns and fish with the batter and deep-fry in very hot oil. Place a portion of noodles into large individual serving bowls and place a prawn and a piece of fish on top of each. Bring the stock to a rapid boil, season to taste with salt and freshly ground white pepper and pour into the bowls. Chop the spring onions and use as garnish.

Zaru Ubon (chilled wheat noodles)

250 g wheatflour noodles
2 sheets nori (seaweed)
20 mm knob fresh ginger
½ clove garlic
2 spring onions

Sauce for dipping:
300 ml dashi
75 ml mirin
75 ml Japanese soya sauce
1 teaspoon sugar
salt to taste
pinch monosodium glutamate

Bring a large saucepan of water to a rapid boil and add the noodles. Cook until tender (approximately 2–3 minutes), then transfer to a colander and rinse under cold running water until the noodles are quite cold. Drain thoroughly before arranging portions on to serving plates. Toast the seaweed under a hot grill until crispy, then crumble over the noodles. Grate the ginger and garlic and slice the spring onions very finely. Mix these together and place into small individual side dishes. Add a little sauce to each dish and use as a dip for the noodles.

To make the sauce; pour the dashi, mirin and soya sauce into a saucepan and bring to the boil. Add sugar, salt and monosodium glutamate, stir to blend thoroughly and allow to simmer for 1 minute. Set aside to cool before using.

Oshiruko *(red bean dessert)*

200 g azuki (red beans)
200 g sugar
pinch of salt
50 g seedless raisins

Wash the beans thoroughly under cold running water, then drain well and place into a saucepan. Add sufficient cold water to cover the beans and bring to the boil. Cover the pan, lower heat and allow to cook slowly until the beans are tender, approximately 50 minutes. Remove the cover, add the sugar and salt and stir to blend thoroughly. Cook for a further 10 minutes, stirring frequently. Serve immediately or allow to cool, place in the refrigerator and serve cold with vanilla ice-cream.

Green Tea Ice-Cream

250 ml double cream
2 eggs
25 g cornstarch
2 teaspoons green tea powder
250 ml milk
75 g sugar

Partially whip the cream and place in a refrigerator for at least 30 minutes before using. Break the eggs into a mixing bowl and beat lightly, then add the cornstarch and green tea powder and stir well. Pour the milk into a saucepan, add the sugar and bring to the boil. Immediately lower heat and simmer until the sugar has completely dissolved, then add the egg mixture and continue to cook slowly, stirring continuously, until the mixture thickens. Remove from heat and allow to cool then fold in the partially whipped cream. Place in the refrigerator and chill slightly. Remove and whisk well, then place in the freezer compartment for 15–20 minutes. Remove, whisk again and replace in the freezer. Repeat this process three or four times, then arrange in mounds and return to the freezer to set hard before serving.

Chimaki *(rice cakes in bamboo leaves)*

100 g glutinous rice
25 g sugar
$\frac{1}{4}$ teaspoon green colouring
4 bamboo leaves

Place the rice in a saucepan and cover with cold water. Bring to the boil, then lower heat, cover the pan and cook slowly until the rice is tender and most of the water has been absorbed (the rice should remain sticky). Add the sugar and the green colouring and stir to blend thoroughly. Remove from the heat, shape the rice into four small mounds, wrap each in a bamboo leaf and secure with toothpicks. Place on a wooden rack over boiling water and steam for 5 minutes, then serve immediately.

Index

Other books published in this series:
'Tastes' of Hong Kong, Singapore, Malaysia, Philippines & Thailand